Managing Stress

Learning to Pace Your Chase Through Life

Dale R. Olen, Ph.D.

A Life Skills Series Book

JODA Communications, Ltd.
Milwaukee, Wisconsin

Editor: Carolyn Kott Washburne
Design and Layout: Chris Roerden and Associates

ISBN 1-56583-003-2

Published by: JODA Communications, Ltd.
10125 West North Avenue
Milwaukee, WI 53226

PRINTED IN THE UNITED STATES OF AMERICA

Table of Contents

Introduction
to the
Life Skills Series

Nobody gets out alive! It isn't easy navigating your way through life. Your relationships, parents, marriage, children, job, school, church, all make big demands on you. Sometimes you feel rather ill-equipped to make this journey. You feel as if you have been tossed out in the cold without even a warm jacket. Life's journey demands considerable skill. Navigating the sometimes smooth, other times treacherous journey calls for a wide variety of tools and talents. When the ride feels like a sailboat pushed by a gentle breeze, slicing through the still waters, you go with the flow. You live naturally with the skills already developed.

But other times (and these other times can make you forget the smooth sailing), the sea turns. The boat shifts violently, driven by the waves' force. At those stormy moments, you look at your personal resources, and they just don't seem sufficient.

Gabriel Marcel, the French philosopher, wrote that the journey of life is like a spiral. The Greeks, he observed, viewed life as *cyclical*—sort of the same old thing over and over. The seasons came, went, and came again. History repeated itself. The Hebrews, on the other hand, saw life as *linear*—a pretty straight march toward a goal. You begin at the Alpha point and end at Omega. It's as simple as that.

Marcel combined the two views by capturing the goal-oriented optimism of the Hebrews and the sobering reality of the Greeks' cycles. Life has its ups and downs, but it always moves forward.

To minimize the *downs* and to make the most of the *ups*, you need **Life Skills**. When you hike down the Grand Canyon, you use particular muscles in your back and legs. And when you trudge up the Canyon, you use other muscles. So too with life skills. You call on certain skills when your life spirals down, such as the skill of defeating depression and managing stress. When your life is on an upswing, you employ skills like thinking reasonably and meeting life head on.

This series of books is about the skills you need for getting through life. To get from beginning to end without falling flat on your face and to achieve some dignity and some self-satisfaction, you need **basic** life skills. These include:

1. Accepting yourself.
2. Thinking reasonably.
3. Meeting life head on.

With these three life skills mastered to some degree, you can get a handle on your life. Now, if you want to build from there, you are going to need a few more skills. These include:

4. Communicating.
5. Managing stress.
6. Being intimate.
7. Resolving conflict.
8. Reducing anger.
9. Overcoming fear.
10. Defeating depression.

If you have these ten skills up and running in your life, you are ready to face yourself, your relationships, your parents, your marriage, your children, your job and even God with the hope of handling whatever comes your way. Without these skills, you are going to bump into one stone wall after another. These skills don't take away the problems, the challenges and the hard times. But they do help you dig out of life's deep trenches and more fully *enjoy* the good times.

Life Skills can be learned. You have what it takes to master each of these skills–even if you feel you don't have the tiniest bit of the skill right now. But nobody can develop the skill for you. You have to take charge and develop it yourself. Your family, friends and community may be able to help you, but you are the center at which each skill has to start. Here is all you need to begin this learning process:

- Awareness.
- The desire to grow.
- Effort and practice.

Awareness begins the process of change. You have to notice yourself, watch your behavior and honestly face your strengths and weaknesses. You have to take stock of each skill and of the obstacles in you that might inhibit its growth.

Once you recognize the value of a skill and focus on it, you have to want to pursue it. The critical principle here, one you will see throughout this series, is *desire*. Your desire will force you to focus on the growing you want to do and keep you going when learning comes hard.

Finally, your *effort and practice* will make these **Life Skills** come alive for you. You can do it. The ten books in the **Life Skills Series** are tools to guide and encourage your progress. They are my way of being with you–cheering your efforts. But without your practice, what you find in these books will wash out to sea.

Working on these ten **Life Skills** won't get you through life without any scars. But the effort you put in will help you measure your life in more than years. Your life will be measured in the zest, faith, love, honesty and generosity you bring to yourself and your relationships.

I can hardly wait for you to get started!

Chapter One

What Is Stress?

Trying to shove the round peg into the square hole, that's stress! Your car and the city bus vying for the same space at the stoplight, that's stress! Your alarm clock going off this morning during that most pleasant dream, that's stress! The shower spitting out cold water because your daughter got to the bathroom before you did, that's stress!

What makes all these events stressful? Simple. Their parts do not *fit together*, and *you want them to*. You try on your jeans from last summer. Uh-oh! Those pants and your waist don't fit. And you want them to! If you didn't care, or if you hoped they wouldn't fit, you would not have stress. But, you say, how can you hope your pants wouldn't fit? I can tell you haven't had to work on the weight issue. You hope they don't fit because you *lost* 10 pounds during the winter and your jeans are now way too big. Hallelujah! Here's a situation where things don't fit, but instead of causing you stress, it brings you joy. That's because to have stress, you need to *want* two nonfitting things to fit.

The chairperson said the meeting would start at 10 A.M. You hustle to get there on time, and do. That all fits together – meeting scheduled for 10 A.M., you are present. But the meeting doesn't start

9

because the chairperson isn't there. At 10:30 she strolls in and begins. She doesn't apologize or explain her tardiness. Now you're stressed. Your time and her time don't fit together. And you want them to. Then your sense of acknowledging one's mistakes (her apologizing for being late) and her lack of apology also don't fit. And you want them to. That's additional stress.

Imagine how many things don't fit in your life. It's unbelievable. Your time doesn't fit with the demands on your time. The level of noise in your environment doesn't fit with your desire for peace and quiet. Your work demands don't match your desires for leisure. The amount of housework doesn't fit well with the demands of your children to play with them. A lot doesn't fit in your world. These are the general, always present non-fits in your life.

Then there are the tiny, daily elements that don't fit well, either. The amount of cereal you put in your bowl doesn't fit with the size of the bowl. The coffee spots on your shirt don't fit your executive image. Your idea of what your daughter should wear to school doesn't fit with her idea. The dog doing his duty *inside* the screen door doesn't fit with your idea of a clean house.

All these non-fitting experiences loom around and within you daily. They offer the material for major stress in your life. But you add the crowning piece. You want – in fact, you insist – that these non-fitting pieces of reality fit and work together in harmony. Now, there's your stress. You want what doesn't fit to fit. If it continues not fitting, you attempt to force it. The harder you try, the more stress you create for yourself.

At the other end of stress lies *harmony*. Think of those moments when peace reigns, when you feel stress-free. I know they may seem rare, but they do exist. There is a cartoon that shows a man sitting in his living room and in the background his wife passes by. He looks up from his paper with a surprised and quizzical look and says, "What the hell was *that*? Something just swept over me – like contentment or something." I'm sure you have had those moments as well.

Perhaps you were driving home from work. Everything had gone well during the day. All your projects were on time and running smoothly. Your family was doing fine. The sun was shining. You felt content. Everything was in its place and all was well with your world. When all is in harmony, all is in its place, then you have peace of mind.

Tiny moments of fittingness occur for you on a daily basis. But you may not notice them or celebrate them the way you do when things don't fit together. Your two-mile jog fit well with your active lungs and heart. Your breakfast food fit well with your hungry stomach. Your creative ideas matched well with your need to get that report done. Your partner's embrace snuggled right up to your desire for his or her love. Your warm bed complemented your body's craving for sleep. Appreciating what *does* fit, enjoying it and celebrating it, helps you balance all the non-fitting aspects of your life. In fact, the more you appreciate the harmony in your life, the less likely will be your demands that the non-harmonious parts fit together perfectly. You will more easily enjoy what already fits.

Principle 1

Stress comes from three sources: personal, interpersonal and environmental.

You find stress within yourself. You also face it in the interactions between you and other people. And, finally, you encounter it in the dynamic world around you. Identifying these sources of your stress helps you overcome it.

Personal stress has *physical* and *mental* aspects. Physically, stress occurs when you put things into your body that don't belong there, such as fats, sugars, nicotine and liquor in excess. Further stress results when your body – made to move and be active – sits much of the day and gets no exercise. Mentally, stress happens when you demand that reality be the same as your expectations of it. When you insist that the real world match your beliefs of how it ought to be but you can't make it so, then stress will fill your being.

Interpersonal stress arises when conflicts occur between you and another person, when you move toward deeper intimacy with another or when you attempt to move away from that person. Stress can happen when you meet new people, when you focus too much on impressing or pleasing people, when you work with difficult people and when you feel one-down in a relationship.

Environmental stress lays its burden on you with all the external pressures you feel. Time is a major burden. There is usually never enough of it. Balancing areas of your life becomes increasingly difficult. Trying to make your work life, home life, leisure and relational life fit together can feel nearly impossible. Juggling *roles* as a career woman, wife, mother, friend and volunteer can cause much inner conflict. Finally, living in a society marked by pollution, noise, prejudice and violence increases the stress you encounter daily.

You know what stress is and how it affects you. Now let's figure out ways of reducing it in your life.

Chapter Two

Principles and Tools for Managing Stress

Fortunately, you have a variety of weapons in your personal arsenal to combat stress. Although stress pervades your 20th-century life, it can be managed. In fact, it can be brought under control quite handily. The tools are there. All that's needed is your application and your effort. I will identify the ways you can handle stress; I am confident you will supply the effort.

Managing Stress Physically

Your body was created to *move*. When it doesn't get an opportunity to do so, it becomes stressed. It is not in harmony with itself. Your body was also created to take in certain foods in order to fuel it. Food gives the body energy, strengthening it, healing it, protecting it from illness. But not all foods serve the body in these positive ways. Some foods hurt and destroy the body. Some liquids do so as well. Other toxins enter the body and harm it. These elements do not fit well with your body. They cause *distress*.

Physical stress quietly underlies all the other stressors in your life. Because it is so fundamental to all your stress, let's discuss it first. You may not always feel it or notice it. It's like the basement of the great mansion on the hill. You don't really pay much attention to it. But it's there, supporting the massive structure above.

To bring your stress under control, you need to begin with your body. First, you want to assess what you eat and take into your body. Second, you want to look at how much physical activity you get, and what kind of activity it is. Then – and here's the important part – you will need to realize that whatever changes you see as necessary to reducing bodily stress will have to involve *lifestyle changes*.

You cannot decide to cut out ice cream for dessert just until Father's Day. Or you can't say you'll not eat between meals from now until you lose that ten pounds. You need to decide on a way and pattern of living that is consistent and constant. You are trying to make decisions to change that will stick with you for the rest of your life. I am not suggesting you deny yourself ice cream until your deathbed. I am saying you need to make choices, sensible and prudent choices, that balance your need for eating nutritiously with your desire for the pleasures of taste. You need to make decisions that blend a physically active life with a sedentary lifestyle.

Lifestyle changes become embedded in you. You have to do them regularly. Many people have gotten into jogging as a lifestyle choice. No matter the weather, they are out there doing their two miles a day. Without that two-mile run they feel incomplete. They have to do it. People who have sworn off sugar on a regular basis feel uneasy when they eat a dessert at a wedding. It makes them physically and psychologically uncomfortable thinking about that sugar going into their clean system.

Let me share a personal example of a lifestyle change. A number of years ago my teeth and gums were going downhill fast. My dentist talked with me about using dental floss. I never had used it before. But I began doing so because my gums were in bad shape. I had to do it or possibly face surgery. That was motivation enough. Soon I got into the habit. Ever since, I floss every night. Occasionally, I run out of floss or forget it on a trip, and when that happens, it bothers me. My mouth feels dirty. I sense a little anxiety about decay and gum disease. That's a lifestyle change, the kind you may need to make in your life to reduce the stress you experience.

Don't get me wrong. I'm not saying that by using dental floss you will reduce your stress! I am saying that changes about eating and physical activity which increase your health and reduce your stress need to be lifestyle changes. They need to be changes that stick. They need to be consistent behaviors, without which you feel incomplete and uncomfortable.

Principle 2

Make a commitment to create harmony between your body and what you put into it.

No, I'm not going to talk with you about going on a diet. Nor will I tell you how important it is to eliminate as much sugar, salt and fat as you can from your diet. I certainly am not going to recommend drinking powders or taking weight-loss pills. What I do want to tell you is to forget about weight loss as your goal and concentrate instead on eating *properly*.

If weight loss is your goal, then you will tend to starve-eat, starve-eat your way through life – feeling stressed the entire time. I've watched people try to lose weight. I have tried. It causes stress! Every morning, just before you get on the scale, anxiety builds. You get on and "think" you may have lost half a pound. However, if you rock just a little backwards on the scale, it looks like you actually lost a whole pound. Then you rock forward, and your heart sinks, because now it seems like you gained two pounds overnight.

You think strange and stressful thoughts when you're trying to "lose weight." Before weighing, you think, "I shouldn't weigh myself after my shower because my hair will be wet and I might weigh more." Certainly, "I should go to the toilet and eliminate as much waste material as I can before weighing." When you eat a cracker during the day (which is off your diet), you wonder: "I'll probably gain a pound now. Oh, my God. I just blew my entire diet. I will probably spiral into major obesity." You go out to a restaurant with your friends and scour the menu for the least caloric meal. All during the meal, in your mind, you are adding up your calories, mathematically calculating whether you are over or under. Stress abounds.

Finally, you reach your goal weight. How neat! Then you think if you just took off another two or three pounds, you'd really be in shape. More stress, because those next couple of pounds come off with great difficulty. Or you go in the other direction. Now that the weight is off, you get a reward – dessert at your next meal. Over time you eat more desserts, more chips and cookies (it's Christmas, you know). The weight returns, and you feel miserable as you see it inching back. More stress.

To reduce your stress, and perhaps your weight as well, don't focus on weight loss as your goal. Instead, pay attention to eating well for the sake of health. Decide to eat for the good of your body. If you just won a $50,000 car (wouldn't that be nice?) and the dealer told you to put only premium gas in it, that's exactly what you would do. You would pay the extra fifteen cents a gallon to keep the car running perfectly. You would change the oil every 2,000 miles and make sure all your fluids were topped off with the best brands on the market.

Well, you inherited a body worth a lot more than a $50,000 car. I know how tempting it is to fill it with junk, but concentrate as best as you can on what a valuable piece of machinery your body is. It will function well and long only if it is fed high octane foods. By giving

your body what it *needs* to function well, you create the *fit* you need
to live without stress.

Along with eating the "right" foods, you will also want to attend
to the *amount* of food you consume. I know that many people turn to
food when they feel stressed. It relaxes them, they claim. But while
it immediately gratifies that restless need, it increases the amount of
stress on the body itself. When you pour premium gas into your sports
car, you can only put in so much. When it is filled, the gas runs out
if you keep on pumping. Your body's gas tank, or stomach, has a
different kind of wall than the car's. It expands to meet the amount
of food being sent in. It then also has the wonderful capacity of storing
the overflow in fat, sending it throughout the body.

With the car, you know when enough is enough. The gas
overflows. With your body, *you* need to decide to stop. The general
rule of thumb has been to eat only when you are biologically hungry,
not just for pleasure or in response to stress. And to eat only as much
as you need to take care of your hunger. Now, that's a whole lot easier
to say than do. This is where your effort comes in.

Let me suggest that you make some practical decisions about
what you are eating. But make your decisions about only one or two
things that you think are possible. For instance, decide to eat fruit for
snacks instead of chips. Have one piece of toast for breakfast instead
of two. Drink a glass of orange juice instead of the second cup of
coffee. Add broccoli to your supper fare at least once a week. In other
words, just get going in a positive direction. Take a couple of small
steps at first, aiming at developing a healthful eating style for this
valuable body of yours. Concentrate on your health rather than your
weight. Eat nutritious foods and cut down the volume.

By doing any two of these things you make a major lifestyle
change that will increase the length and quality of your life. And it
will eliminate one of the major sources of stress – the non-fit of
substances in your body that should not be there.

Principle 3

**Make a commitment to get physically active
because your body needs it.**

When my wife and I first got our beagle hound, Sidney, the dog breeder gave us an operating manual and a set of instructions. The first and most important order was: "Take your dog for a walk every day." We've tried, but that's a pretty demanding rule. Many days we succumb to the snow, rain and cold. Other days we give in to our own laziness. Yet we try to get him out there as much as possible. When Sidney walks, he is in harmony with himself. It is crystal clear to us that this dog was made to walk. In fact, when we say the word "walk" in passing conversation, he immediately springs to action, wagging his tail and scratching at the door.

That dog's body was made for action. So is yours. You may not feel the impulse to scratch at the door when someone suggests a walk, but your body craves activity. Without it, everything in you begins to tighten up and atrophy. In the "old days" people didn't have to worry about physical movement. They were going from dawn to dusk, working the fields, milking the cows, cleaning up after 10 kids. Now we sit at computers, behind desks and in conference rooms exercising our minds, not our bodies. That kind of behavior does not fit well with the drive in the body to move. The result is a constant, low-grade stress. You might not notice it, but it's there.

To make some lifestyle changes or at least strengthen those that promote physical activity, you need to look at three areas:

1. Vigorous activity.
2. Muscle building and toning activity.
3. Stretching activity.

First, you want to get moving with *vigor*. Your heart and lungs need to be challenged regularly. Most experts recommend that you increase your pulse rate significantly for at least 20 minutes, three times a week. Vigorous exercise means doing something continuously for that 20 minutes, such as jogging, bike riding (without a lot of coasting), swimming or aerobics. While walking is a great exercise, it has to be done briskly to increase your pulse rate. Tennis and golf, unfortunately, don't do the job. Too much starting and stopping. If you want to get going on vigorous exercise, do two things. If you haven't had a physical exam for some time, go get one. This is a good idea anyway for beginning your lifelong process of reducing the stress in your life.

Next, start slowly. Begin by walking or riding your bike for short distances. Build up speed and time as you go along. Just get into the swing of it. Don't overdo it, because exercise will then become a burden to you. If you try to do too much too quickly, it will seem like a job that has to be done. You want to let yourself "get hooked." By that I don't mean becoming a fanatic. Just give yourself time to let your exercise become part of your lifestyle.

Second, you want to *build* and *tone* your muscles. Your muscles were made to move about. You notice that when you sit in the same position for a long time, you begin to stiffen. Your muscles are feeling stressed, because non-movement doesn't fit with their need to move. On the other hand, you need not become a muscle-bound person. This would be overdoing it. But consistent muscle work will strengthen your body. It will help you fight the traumas that affect your body, such as accidents, falls, illnesses and disease. Many people do muscle work to tone their bodies as well. They attempt to turn their fat into muscle. They do it for the sake of appearance as well as health.

According to the body experts, strenuous activity should be done a minimum of 20 minutes, three times a week. Using weight machines best achieves the goal of strengthening most of your large muscle groups, and it offers a systematic approach to making sure your whole body gets a workout. Coaches tell you *not* to lift weights or work the machines every day. You should have at least one day off between workouts to rest your muscles.

Right now you're probably feeling some stress as I describe these exercise routines. You're concerned about the amount of time you'll have to spend. With vigorous activity and strenuous exercise you're already up to 40 minutes a day, three days a week. And that's minimum. I know. That's why I'm suggesting that you start easily and slowly. I'd start with the vigorous exercises first. It's so important to get your heart and lungs working at full capacity. But there is an exercise you can use to achieve two results. Aerobic exercises satisfy your daily requirements for both vigorous and muscle work. Aerobics work many of your muscles, and they certainly challenge your heart. At the end of such an exercise period your body feels spent, but whole.

Third, you want to do *stretching* exercises. Stretching keeps you loose, flexible and agile. It allows your internal body parts to function more freely. Kareem Abdul Jabbar claimed that he was able to keep playing professional basketball at such a competitive level because he had done stretching exercises religiously from high school on.

How frequently should you do these exercises? Sit down for this one. Twenty minutes, six times a week. Put all three of these areas of exercise together – vigorous activity, muscle building and toning, and stretching – and you could be spending an hour a day, four or five days a week. That's right. But again, remember that I'm suggesting you start slowly and do what you can. Just get into it at some level. When you turn these activities into lifestyle issues, you will find the time to take care of your body and become fit.

The body needs activity. It needs to be worked and challenged. It needs strength and flexibility. When these needs are met, your body feels free from stress. Furthermore, with a stress-free body you more easily handle all the other stresses occurring in your daily life. Stress management starts with your body. Eat healthful foods and get your body moving well, and you take the first major step toward developing the skill of managing your stress.

Principle 4

Practice relaxing your body regularly.

If you keep your body relaxed and calm, you also keep your stress under control. A relaxed body overcomes the tension created by stress. But relaxation does not come at the snap of a finger. It takes sustained practice to create a physical state of quiet and peace.

If you're like many people, you know about relaxation techniques but you try them only when you are at the height of your stress tolerance. You can't take the stress any longer, so you think, "Ah, I'll try a relaxation exercise." You do it once. It doesn't help much. And you forget about it. If you want relaxation to help you manage your stress, then you need to get in the *habit* of practicing it. You want to build your relaxing skills so that when you hit the crisis, your body will know how to enter into a relaxing and peaceful mode. It will be able to act against the stress by calming itself and setting the stage for your mind to calm down as well.

I want to teach you an easy relaxation process that works if you do it regularly. Herb Benson, M.D., a cardiologist from Boston, developed a process called the "Relaxation Response." (*The Relaxation Response,* William Morrow, 1975.) In a way, he reinvented the wheel. This process in various forms has been practiced by people for years, even centuries. But Benson brought it up to date and created wonderful practical applications for people suffering from heart disease, cancer and chronic physical pain. The applications for people suffering from psychological and emotional stress are just as useful. His approach is simple to learn and needs only your willingness to hang in there and do it.

Steps for the Relaxation Response

1. Stretch briefly and loosen up your muscles. Rub the tension out of your face and especially around your eyes. You have hundreds of tiny muscles around your eyes and throughout your face that tighten up under stress. Simply rubbing out that tension begins the relaxation process. Sit quietly, preferably with both feet on the ground, and close your eyes. If you get dizzy by keeping your eyes closed, then leave them open and focus on something on the floor in front of you.

2. Take slow, normal breaths, paying attention to your breathing in and breathing out. Notice the effect your breathing has on your body.

3. Find a word or a phrase you like, and repeat it to yourself every time you breathe out. This is called a "mantra." Mantras are special phrases used in many Eastern meditation rituals to help people slow down their thought processes and go into trance-like states. The phrase you decide on should be short, usually no more than seven words, preferably three to five words. The phrase should not be longer than your out-breath. If you have a strong religious orientation, you might choose a religious phrase, such as "The Lord is my shepherd." Or you can choose something you value, such as the phrase "Love and peace." If you cannot think of any phrase, then use "One, two, three, four." Once you decide on a phrase, keep it. You do not want to change it frequently.

   Now that you have your phrase, pay attention again to your breathing in and breathing out. As you do this, begin repeating your phrase within yourself every time you breathe out.

4. As you breathe and say your phrase, other thoughts will enter your mind. Acknowledge them, passively disregard them and return to your breathing and to your phrase. Some days you

will feel free from outside thoughts; other days you will feel plagued by them. Don't be concerned. Just return to your breathing and repeat your phrase.

5. Do this Relaxation Response at least *once* a day for 10 to 20 minutes. "Oh my gosh," you're thinking. "First, he wants us to exercise for an hour a day. Now he wants us to find another 10 to 20 minutes to sit and repeat a phrase." Your stress may be increasing just by reading this section. I hope not. I am sharing with you what works in reducing stress. Again, at first I want to encourage you to take small steps. Pick and choose what you can do. Then do it. Dr. Benson originally wanted people to do this exercise *twice* a day. I used to encourage that, but stopped when I realized I myself was doing it only once a day. But I believe once a day will get you very similar results.

6. Try not to do the Relaxation Response right after you eat because you will tend to fall asleep. The idea of this process is not to sleep but to relax. In fact, you will often notice an increase in energy after you do this exercise.

7. Have no goals in mind when doing this exercise. If you try to make yourself relax or stop worrying about something, you may well increase your stress. You need to think about these 10 minutes a day as time to do nothing but breathe and say your phrase. Some days you will feel more relaxed when you are finished; other days you may not. Some days you will have more disturbing thoughts filling your mind; other days no thoughts will enter. Just let yourself be with your breathing and your phrase. This is a time for you to simply sit quietly, do nothing and think nothing.

There it is. Simple, right? Dr. Benson and his group in Boston have documented the physical effects of this practice on people with high blood pressure and with chronic pain. I have seen the effects on people psychologically and emotionally. Doing this exercise regu-

larly causes an amazing thing to happen. With two to six months of
daily practice, you attach to your breathing and to that phrase a state
of peacefulness and rest that can almost be called up on demand.

By doing this exercise day in and day out, you generally feel
peaceful and quiet as you are doing it. For those 10 minutes, at least,
you calm down. Over time, those 10 minutes tend to spread out. You
feel calmer for longer periods of time.

Then you find an interesting thing happening. Throughout your
day, especially when you feel stressed, by recalling your phrase and
taking a couple of conscious slow breaths, you experience the same
state of peace you created when doing the Relaxation Response. The
feelings of calm and peace become attached to your phrase and
breath. So whenever you consciously return to your breathing and
your phrase, you regain a sense of peace.

I encourage you to try the Relaxation Response. And stick with
it. Like anything, the more you practice it, the more impact it will
have on your life. You can also learn more about it by reading Herbert
Benson's book, *The Relaxation Response*.

Managing Stress Mentally

You cause your own stress, in large part, by the way you think.
The perspective you take, the interpretations you make and the
conclusions you come to – all in your mind – make or break the stress
"pac-men" that can eat you up. So to reduce your stress, you first want
to realize that it is mostly in your mind. By changing your thought
patterns, you change your stress levels. I will identify for you the
kinds of thoughts that cause you stress, and the thoughts you can use
to reduce your stress. To understand more fully how to work with
your mind in reducing stress, I suggest you read the book in the **Life
Skills Series** called *Thinking Reasonably*.

Principle 5

Develop a sense of confidence in your ability to cope with and reduce stress.

In every step of your life, your thoughts and your attitudes precede your behavior and your feelings. The more positive your attitudes, the more likely your behavior results in positive outcomes. If you think successfully, you act successfully. If you watched the last several Olympics on television, you may have noticed the sports psychologists working on mental imagery with the athletes. They put the athletes in trance-like states of deep relaxation. Then, they helped the athletes paint verbal pictures of going through their events successfully. The psychologists wanted the athletes to picture what they were about to do. By seeing themselves in their minds tumbling, running or skating in peak performance, the athletes would more likely perform accordingly.

Your mind creates the self-fulfilling prophecy. If you anticipate failure, you will probably achieve failure. If you anticipate success, you will have a much better chance of acting successfully.

With stress, you want to create self-fulfilling prophecies that tell you of your ability to handle the difficulties of life. Although you will suffer occasions of stress, you will be better able to feel in charge of those occasions. You will know you can relieve the stress. It is not bigger than you.

Often you may feel as though you have no control over the stresses in your life. So you remain a slave to them, allowing them to continually bombard you. You become a *victim* of the stresses. You keep behaving in the same ways, pulled along by the difficulties of life, feeling that you have no other choices.

Sheikh Nasrudin felt the same way, according to a story told by Swami Muktananda in his book *Where Are You Going?* (SYDA Foundation, 1989). Apparently the Sheikh saw people buying chili peppers at the market and decided to buy some himself. He bought two kilos of the eye-watering, hot, hot peppers. He sat under a tree and began eating them. They were terrible. They burned his mouth and tongue, and tasted awful. But he kept eating them. A man noticed him continuing to eat the chilies and asked why he was doing so. The Sheikh replied that he saw other people buying them, thought they were good for eating and so got some himself. He thought if he just kept eating them, they would eventually start tasting better.

The man explained that the chilies were to be eaten in very small quantities and usually with other food. The Sheikh nodded and kept on eating, his distress mounting. The other man couldn't believe his eyes. In astonishment he said, "Why don't you stop if they burn so much?" Sheikh Nasrudin said, "I bought these chilies and I have to finish them. I'm not eating chilies any longer, I'm eating my money!"

The Sheikh could think in only one way. He could see no other *choices*, even though the other man offered him one. His mind was set. If he had paid to eat this food, then he must eat the food, no matter how terrible it was. So his stress continued.

You need not operate like Sheikh Nasrudin. If stress has grabbed hold of you, you can always make other *choices*. You need not continue to respond in the same way. I want to encourage you to work hard on realizing *you* have control over your stresses. You can think differently, see in a new way. You can interfere with your automatic and habitual responses to the life stresses that pull you this way and that.

To live in today's action-packed world, filled with non-fitting parts, you need mental toughness. James Bond or Indiana Jones can serve as role models for mental toughness. While you might not want to get into their lifestyles on a daily basis, their confidence and assurance in the face of stress exemplify the confidence needed to handle the stress you experience daily. No matter what happens to them, they are confident they can find a way out. I know you don't live in the movies where the actors can do 20 takes in order to get it right. But the *attitude* of tough confidence in the face of stress is something I'd like you to emulate.

Think of yourself, then, as the controller and master of your own destiny. No matter what happens to you or around you, you have *choices*. You are never enslaved to respond in only one way. You don't have to keep eating the chilies. You can confidently decide to respond differently. You can continue to hope for a better future, for a more relaxed and peaceful time. Getting your mind in a positive, active, choice-making frame will free you from much of the stress that tugs at your soul.

Principle 6

Realize that you cause your own stress by thinking suffering thoughts. To reduce stress, then, learn to think healing thoughts.

You suffer in your mind, not in your body. Your body can feel pain, but your mind takes care of your suffering. By identifying the thoughts that cause you grief, you take the first important steps toward stress management. You have certain "demons" that keep popping up in your thinking. By naming them, you begin taking power over them. These are the villains that cause you stress. These "afflicting thoughts" need to be ferreted out, isolated from your other healthy thoughts and replaced with less suffering thoughts that yield peace and contentment.

Next are the main culprits, the thoughts that cause stress—with their counterparts, the healing thoughts that bring harmony and calm.

THOUGHTS THAT CAUSE STRESS	THOUGHTS THAT CAUSE PEACE
1. Demanding, insisting	1. Wishing, hoping, accepting
2. Rigid	2. Flexible, tolerant
3. Perfectionist	3. Willing to err
4. Judgmental	4. Descriptive
5. Interpretive (especially negatively)	5. Information-seeking, giving benefit of the doubt
6. Negative, pessimistic	6. Positive, optimistic
7. Comparative	7. Unifying, seeking similarities
8. Competitive	8. Cooperative
9. Serious	9. Light-hearted, humorous
10. Resenting, begrudging	10. Forgiving
11. Regretting the past	11. Mindful of present
12. Worrying about the future	12. Focused on now
13. Violent, hateful	13. Peaceful, loving

Imagine your life if you were filled only with "thoughts that cause stress." You'd be miserable. Nothing would ever fit right. Everything would appear serious and dark. The tension in your body would cry out for release because of your insistence that all must proceed perfectly.

Let's suppose you are going to the theater to see a play. On the way you try beating another car to the center lane of the expressway (competitive). You get upset with the truck hogging two lanes (demanding). You get to the parking structure and complain about the way it was built (negative). You grouse at the ticket-taker because she is too slow (rigid). You think how incompetent she is, probably a high school drop-out (judgmental, interpretive).

Afterwards, you grumble about how this play wasn't half as good as the last one you saw – which wasn't very good anyway (comparative). On the way home, you wish you had never come (regretful). Finally, you get very angry with your spouse for dragging you along (violent). Whew! Nice night at the theater. Think you'd have any stress after your evening out?

Now let's look at the same scene as if you are entertaining peaceful thoughts. You'd first enjoy just getting out with your spouse. If some people on the expressway are in a hurry, fine. Let them have the center lane (accepting). Trucks will be trucks and at times will take two lanes (flexible). You see the parking structure as intriguing and a challenge. It's actually sort of funny (humorous). The ticket-taker is slow, but it's because she's greeting everyone personally (descriptive). You appreciate the acting and the scenery even though the plot is developing a little slowly (positive). You see it as a good production in its own right (mindful of present). You thank your spouse for thinking of going to the play. It was good just enjoying something together (peaceful, unifying, cooperative). What a pleasant night at the theater. You feel relaxed and content.

If you find yourself grumbling internally, failing to enjoy the delightful aspects of life, feeling up-tight way too often, then look for some or all of the "thoughts that cause stress." They will certainly be lurking in the basement of your mind. Challenge them and replace them with "thoughts that cause peace." You can plainly see that the *event* – in this case going to the play – does not have the power to create stress. Your *thoughts* will do you in or help you out. This area needs your hard work. Keep seeing the world in a flexible, descriptive, humorous and peaceful way. You will find more harmony in it – and within yourself – than you ever might have imagined.

Managing Interpersonal Stress

What causes you the most stress? Chances are you'll answer that question by pointing to another person or to a situation involving other people. You break up with a boyfriend. You feel shut out by a neighbor. Your daughter seems more defiant lately. Your boss is obnoxious. Your neighbor is butting in again. Your sister is very sick. Your golfing partner cheats on strokes. Your business partner isn't pulling his fair share of the load.

These interpersonal situations cause intense levels of stress. They catch you up emotionally. They pervade your consciousness. Just when they seem to settle down, they pop up again. Your ability to handle interpersonal relationships smoothly determines the amount of stress you will feel on a daily basis. Throughout your life you have learned ways of responding to people. Some of those ways work and others do not. To look at all the ways to create harmony in your relationships would take us far beyond the scope of this book. Yet dealing effectively with your relationships is essential to reducing your stress. I encourage you to read one or all of the following books in the **Life Skills Series:** *Resolving Conflict, Being Intimate* and *Communicating.*

The next three principles will help you interact in a more peaceful, less stressed way.

Principle 7

Learn when to say " no" and when to say " yes."

Going to weddings, parties and occasions you really don't want to go to causes stress. Volunteering to serve on a committee when you just don't have any more time causes stress. Helping your neighbor move when you really want to paint your window frames creates tension. Saying "yes" when you really want to say "no" is a major cause of stress in relationships. Added stress occurs when you do finally say "no" and then feel guilty about it for days.

Suppose your pastor calls and asks if you would please help with the church picnic. You really don't have the time or the interest. But it *is* the pastor. You don't want to disappoint him. He might think less of you. So you say "yes" without being clear with yourself about your own needs and your pastor's need. In fact, you probably aren't even paying attention to what you want. You simply respond to his need.

You want to talk with yourself about this. If you are like me, then you learned years ago to put others before you. It was considered selfish to do something for yourself before you did something for another person. The way I learned it was: "God first. Others second. Me third." If I acted according to that principle, then I got others' approval, God's approval and my own. If I put me ahead of God or others, then I was a bad boy. Today, in one form or another, I hear this philosophy of life a lot.

If you still hold to this belief, then I want you to consider another point of view. The two great commandments of the Christian tradition have been to "Love God with your whole heart and soul. And to love your neighbor as yourself." Many people, I'm afraid, forget the "as yourself" part. This commandment places others and you on the same plane. One does not really take preference over the other. You don't have to sacrifice your needs and desires automatically because someone else needs something from you.

If two friends call and each asks for a favor at the very same time, what would you do? Let's say John asks you to help him break out the concrete in his old patio on Saturday. At the same time Tom asks you to help him lay sod on his front lawn on Saturday. You have only the morning available because your spouse's youngest sister is getting married in the afternoon. And you have to go to that. How would you decide which friend to help?

You would probably make your decision based on which of these two friends seems to have the greatest need for your help at the time. Suppose you learn that John would like to get the patio job finished by mid-summer. His brother will also be helping him on Saturday. Tom, however, has to get his sod laid by Saturday. It was already delivered and cannot remain standing for long or it will die. He has no one else to help him. The decision as to whom you help appears obvious. Tom has the greater need for your services. You choose

Tom and hope that John will understand – which, of course, he does.

When someone asks you to meet one of his or her needs and *you* also have a need, you want to apply the same decision-making process. Only this time the conflict is not between the needs of two friends but between one friend's need and your own need. To see this situation clearly, you can place yourself outside of yourself. You say, "Here's Tom, who has this need to get his sod in. And here's Dale, who has this need to get this manuscript written. Whose need is greater?" If I am objectively able to determine who has the greater need, I will then be able to respond accordingly. In this case I might decide that Tom's need is greater. However, if my publishing deadline is Saturday, then I might recognize my need as greater and do my writing.

Of course, one of the problems here is acknowledging your own needs. Often you will be tempted to minimize your need, afraid you might just be rationalizing. Your fear is that of *being selfish*. If you are afraid of being selfish, you probably are not. You may know some truly selfish people. We often refer to them as sociopathic. They are people without consciences. Their moral principle is: "That is good which gratifies me; that is evil which does not gratify me." If you worry about being selfish, you are far from this distorted moral belief. You need not worry about being selfish if you take care of your needs as well as trying to respond to those of others. You are a worthwhile person who needs care and support just as much as anyone else. Sometimes the only one who can give you such care is yourself.

Principle 8

**Reduce interpersonal stress by making
your needs known.**

If you don't tell people what you need, you won't get your needs met. If you don't get your needs met and you want them met, what you will get is *stress*. Strangely enough, many people don't ask for what they need. They believe they're not supposed to ask, that it's selfish or pushy. They also believe the other person "ought to know" what they need. They "shouldn't have to ask." And in close relationships, they believe that if they have to ask for a need to be filled, the other person's kindness doesn't count as much.

Unfortunately, such people walk through life relatively unhappy, because there isn't a good fit between their needs and their needs being met by others. Stress results.

What if you ask and the other person doesn't respond? You ask your friend to call you tomorrow night after work. She doesn't do it. If you ask a number of times and she still doesn't do it, then you begin feeling some hurt. At that point you need to go to her and address the issue of why she isn't calling you and how you feel about that. You continue to put on the table what's going on for you and what you need from her. You might say, "Karen, I feel bad that you haven't called me for the past week, especially after I asked you several times to do so. When you don't call, I begin wondering all kinds of strange things that end up making me feel hurt. Help me understand how come you haven't called."

She may or may not be able to tell you. But either way you have made your needs known. You have a sense of integrity – a fit between what you need and your ability to ask for it. You cannot totally control whether your need gets met by Karen. She is free to respond or not. But you do control your action. If you need something, you ask for it. If it isn't given to you, then you address the person directly, letting her know how her inaction makes you feel. In this way you take action to reduce your stress.

Most of the interpersonal stress you feel results from unmet needs, either yours or the other person's. When you sense anger in the other person (which is usually very stressful), it signals that he or she has unmet needs. Pay attention to what those are. Simply ask, "What is it you need or want from me that I'm not giving you?" Or if you're hurt or angry, then you say, "Look, I'm angry because I need this from you. And I'm trying hard to get you to see that I need it."

In general, then, you pay attention to needs. And you go toward the other, not away from him or her. You speak about your needs and search for the other's needs. Relationships that run smoothly and have a great deal of harmony are those in which both people feel their needs are being taken care of by the other.

Principle 9

Know when to resolve conflict and when to let it go.

As Kenny Rogers sings in "The Gambler," "You have to know when to hold 'em, and know when to fold 'em." This is true about conflict as well. Some conflicted issues are worth going into, but others are not. In general, psychologists say it is usually better to go into a conflict and try to resolve it directly. While I tend to agree, I also recognize that there are times when it might be more productive to let the conflict go.

In fact, I would say the first effort in a stressed relationship should be to let go of the issue. Notice I didn't say let go of the relationship. No, hold onto the relationship, but let go of the issue. That's an internal act on your part. Suppose the resident male chauvinist makes a sexist remark to whomever will listen. He says, "Women just don't make good executives because they don't think logically." See if you can let the comment roll off your back. Keep it very small in your mind. Perhaps it was a slip of the tongue. He really didn't mean it. Maybe he was just testing your reactions. No big deal.

If he makes no more remarks in the future, then the issue blows away. If the comments continue and they bother you, then directly address the stress developing between the two of you. Perhaps you challenge him on his remarks. He simply makes more of them. You ask him nicely to keep those kinds of comments to himself. He doesn't cooperate. It irritates you whenever you hear him spouting off about women.

He's actually a fairly decent fellow. You could like him except for his narrow view of women. You tried to ignore and let go of his comments. That didn't work for you. Your confrontations, your requests, your demands that he change have not improved the situation. So now you might have to return to your strategy of "letting go." You will need to accept the limitation in this man and appreciate the positives that he brings to work and to your life.

When my children were little, my son, Andy, perfected the skill of upsetting his sister, Amy. He developed an entire repertoire of approaches that hooked her emotionally. My wife and I attempted to instruct her on "letting go" of the stressed situations that arose. We told her, "If you ignore Andy, he will quit doing these things." But no, she continued to enter the conflict, which, as you know, accelerated it rather than stopped it in its tracks.

I think your first effort, then, is to try letting go of conflicts without getting run over. If you feel you will "lose" by letting go, then get into it. If a quick-witted co-worker keeps manipulating you to do all the work, then don't just take it and let it go. Put the brakes on and assert yourself by making your needs known. Also, if you *can't* let go, if you continue being haunted by the words or actions of the other, if the conflict keeps kicking up resentment and anger, then deal with it directly.

But if you can let go of a conflicted issue between you and another, then do it. So the waitress is slow. Let it go. Your business colleague thinks you never told him about some detail of work when you know you did. Let it go. Chalk it up as one of his limitations. Your father whines on the phone, which drives you crazy. Learn to let it go. Accept him as he is.

You see what I'm talking about here, don't you? Flexibility. First try to be flexible, keeping things small in your own mind. (I once said that to a client, and he said: "That shouldn't be hard for me. I have such a small mind anyway." Needless to say, I was working with him on self-esteem.) If you can successfully keep issues small, you won't have to confront the other person. The issue then washes away like pebbles of sand drawn off the beach by the waves.

Managing Environmental Stress

Many things in your environment don't fit well, and therefore cause you stress. However, *time* stands at the head of the list for environmental stressors. Closely behind time comes the heavy demands made on you by the various and perhaps conflicting roles you must play. Let's look at a couple of principles to help you manage your time stresses better and gain needed *balance* in some important aspects of your life.

Principle 10

To manage your time better, you need discipline.

A story is told about the Jesuits, a Catholic religious order of men. To develop character and spiritual values, the Jesuits supposedly performed "spiritual exercises." Many of these exercises involved prayer and meditation. But the exercises also involved *doing* things to reinforce the virtue the men were learning. In order to teach patience, one Jesuit spiritual director called in his student and spilled a cup of pins all over the floor. He told the student to patiently pick them up. The student did so and gave them to the director. The next day the director called in the student and again spilled the pins, asking him to pick them up. This went on for approximately one week, with the student picking up the pins each day. The director was exercising the young man's patience.

After a week, the director thought enough progress had been made. The student was learning patience. How did the director know? Because at the end of the week, the student's teeth were not so tightly clenched, and he even smiled when he left the director's office. What the director did not know was that the student had secretly arranged a pin to sit up nice and tall on the director's chair. Yes, the director sat on it. Whether the student's relaxed jaw and smile signaled patience learned or revenge will never be known!

I'm not sure Jesuits actually spilled pins on the floor to teach patience. But they did believe in *discipline* to teach spiritual and human values. In every religious and value-ladened "way of life" from the East and the West, discipline, structure, ritual and rules have predominated. Yoga masters, swamis, gurus, priests and ministers all demand discipline if their disciples are to achieve the highest states of consciousness and peace.

So it is not surprising that the way for you to manage the chaos and stress in your life is through *discipline*. Putting structure into your life will yield the great prize of harmony. To create that harmony and peace, however, demands a little personal "violence." At least it demands a willingness to act against some of the natural and spontaneous pleasure drives you have.

To put more discipline into your life, you must first decide to resist some of the pleasures you seek at least some of the time. For example, a college student came to see me because for two years in a row he had dropped or flunked classes during the second semester. Each year he started strongly, made it through first semester and then faded as spring came. After exploring all that was going on for him, I realized he simply had no sense of structure in his life. I said to him, "Barney, you need to learn to put some discipline in your life." It was as if I had just told him he had terminal cancer and would die in a few weeks. He actually flinched. The blood ran from his face, his eyes widened, and he mumbled something about not wanting to hear that word.

Barney wanted to have fun. He enjoyed the nights out with the guys, drinking beer and playing poker. When they called, he would quit whatever he was doing and join them. He would begin studying calculus, but someone would call and he'd leave his books, even though he was flunking and had a major test the following morning. You can imagine Barney's stress the next morning as the calculus exam began.

Had he managed his time more effectively by adding a little discipline to his life, Barney would not be spending the summer taking calculus over again. He would have more time now for poker and for beer – though preferably not too much. He may need some discipline in this area too.

To take charge of your time and reduce your stress, you need to look at your pleasures. What pleasures do you take as soon as they present themselves? Do you ever say "no" to them? Can you put off playing with the computer until you get a project finished? Can you set a novel down to finish the laundry? Can you turn off the television after one program to get that desk-work completed?

Take a look at what pleasures you have that cut into your time for other things you have to do. As an exercise, focus on one pleasure and place some limits on it. Or use it as a reward for accomplishing some task you are obliged to do but don't enjoy. Tell yourself, I'll watch the second half of the basketball game on television. But first, I'll pay all the bills or study calculus. In this way you begin taking charge of your time. You feel more in control of your life. The things you have to do will get done. And you still have time for your pleasures.

Once you make a decision to suspend some of your immediate pleasures you can start creating a *plan of action*. Of course, having a plan is one thing and sticking to it is another. But you can't stick to a plan if you don't first have a good one. A good plan is clear and precise. Make your plan specific. Say, "I'm going to exercise immediately after work today for one half-hour. Then I'm going to make supper and afterward work with Jonathan on his homework.

Then Martha and I can spend some time together talking. Finally, I want to watch the second half of the football game."

While this may seem detailed, you need such clarity if you tend not to have any discipline in your life. You can't say, "Sometime today I'll ride the exercise bike." You won't do it. So commit yourself to making a plan of action on a daily basis. Put little rewards in your plan, such as 15 minutes to read a magazine, or take a walk with the dog, or listen to the symphony tape you bought months ago.

Discipline comes from using *force* on yourself and working at it *one day at a time*. When people try to break habits like drinking or smoking, they have to force themselves to stay away from those addictive drugs, and they have to do it one day at a time, often one hour at a time. On the positive side, artists, athletes or students seeking a particular career must force themselves to work hard at their craft. And when things get tough, they tell themselves, "Today, at least, I can do this. I'll worry about tomorrow later."

To take charge of time in your life and reduce the stress it creates, you need to:

1. Identify your immediate pleasures and place some limits on them.
2. Create a specific plan of action.
3. Build into your plan some rewards.
4. Force yourself to stick with your plan.
5. Work your plan one day at a time.

Principle 11

Create a balanced lifestyle.

Getting your life in balance demands some time management, but it also involves knowing *what* you have to balance and knowing the

aspects of your life that need to fit together. There are five:
1. Work.
2. Family/home.
3. Leisure.
4. Public service.
5. Spiritual/religious activity.

Some involvement in each of these areas will afford you a balanced lifestyle. Where do you place most of your psychic energy? The majority of people put it in work or in family/home. The problem arises when you place *all* your energy in one or two areas. If you have no leisure or public service or spiritual growth time, you gradually move toward burnout.

Look at all these areas of your life and see if you aren't overemphasizing one to the detriment of the others. By no means am I suggesting that each of these five areas should receive an equal 20 percent of your time and effort. Clearly, work and home life demand more attention. The point here is not to exclude the other areas. Leisure, some public service and reflective, spiritual time help to balance out the fast-paced lifestyle you live.

Leisure you understand. This is your opportunity to play, rest, relax, let down, be "off." It is a time of no responsibility, no time limits and no demands. It refreshes the body as well as the spirit. It is generally a time of getting filled up rather than filling up others – which you may do most of the time in your work and home life settings.

Public service may be a lesser part of your life unless your work involves such service. But here I'm referring to the voluntary acts that you do to support and build the larger community – the neighborhood, a special interest group, the state or the country. Public service includes such things as writing your legislators regarding your views on various issues. It means organizing the fund drive for your favorite non-profit group, baking cakes for the school bazaar, working on a Saturday morning at the village recycling center or supervising the high school kids' car wash. It could mean getting involved in political action projects, charitable institutions, hospitals, nursing homes or neighborhood programs.

Any involvement you have in the public arena helps broaden your view. It brings balance to the narrow perspective you must have to do your job well and care for your family. It carries you into the larger world on the wings of your own generosity. It feels good for you to contribute, because such action *fits well* with your deepest instincts of caring about the people of the earth.

Spiritual/religious aspects of your life also tend to take up a lesser portion of your time and energy than work and family. But they still remain an important area to develop. Taking time to reflect on the larger purpose of life, the meaning of it all and your part in it will assist you in gaining a fuller perspective. Reading, studying, discussing and thinking about these issues will help you place the other aspects of your life into the big picture. Such a view allows you to challenge your daily, more narrow focus.

Gaining balance in your life by including all five areas to some degree and not overemphasizing one area will also help you handle the various *roles* you must play. Often, your stress may occur because you are wearing too many hats at the same time. You may be a mother, wife, accountant, president of the PTA, daughter to an ailing mother, "counselor" to two friends, gardener, cleaning woman and cook. Too many roles, and they overrun each other. Stress rises again. All of these roles, however, have one thing in common. They all make demands on you. In each of these you must be the *giver*.

That's where the stress comes in. It may be next to impossible to eliminate any of these roles. But maybe you can lessen the demand. Look at each of the roles you play and see if you can't reduce the amount of energy, responsibility and giving you do. Then attempt to put limits on how much you're willing to do. If you really enjoy doing a particular thing, don't reduce it. That's where you *get* something in return for your giving. You get satisfaction and enjoyment.

If you feel the demands of your many roles, the second thing you can do is to make some leisure space. In leisure, you reverse the process. Instead of *giving* all the time, leisure allows you to *receive*. Here's where you need to make your needs known. You will better handle your role of giver if you feel as if you are being filled up as well. Take time, then, to give to yourself. And ask those around you to fill your needs too.

Principle 12

Respect and enjoy the earth and all that is in it.

You may be scratching your head on this principle. "Where did this come from? I thought we were talking about stress. What's respecting the earth got to do with stress management?"

Quite a bit, actually. Most of nature usually works in harmony very well. If you want to see how things fit together, then watch the world around you. Everything in nature depends on other things. Plants need the sunlight. Living creatures need the oxygen given off by the plants. Living creatures provide food for one another, and so on. If you have ever watched a documentary on insects, fish, mammals, plants, caves, mountains, rivers or oceans, you realize how interconnected everything is, and how well it all works together.

For example, in one of the beams on our front porch, I see a robin's nest. All spring the robin worked to build that nest. She found dead straw, twigs and leaves. She laid her eggs and hatched her young – three little guys who poke their heads above the nest's walls hoping Mom will bring home a worm or two. She does. The little ones seem happy, and Mom seems proud. Soon they will fly, finding their own food and home. Watching their activity from my den (when I'm supposed to be writing) brings a certain harmony to me. I feel for the poor worm, but somehow the process of birth, life and death all seem to fit together well.

You can learn about managing stress by experiencing the activity of the earth and its non-human inhabitants. Sit by a waterfall and let it mesmerize you with its power but also with its peacefulness. Do the same at the ocean or lake. The water is well disciplined. It stays within its boundaries (most of the time), lapping the shore with its hypnotic rhythm. Sit at the bottom or top of a mountain (depending on your degree of adventure) and marvel at the strength, stability and history before you. All these happenings announce to you the basics of harmony, of stress management. The elements all fit together. They work as one. Being a part of it allows you to become what nature is, at peace with yourself.

Go to nature as your teacher. You may already do this. You find yourself struggling with a difficult problem. You feel stuck. You tell everyone you're going for a walk. You jump into the car and head for the park, the lake, the hiking trail. Alone, you can take in the sounds and movements of the world around you. You notice little creatures running through the brush. You see and hear the birds above. You feel the cool breeze on your arms. You notice a leaf falling to the ground. No longer are you thinking about your problem. You have been seduced by nature. She calms you. She settles you down and opens you to your creative unconscious. Lo and behold, as you walk along an idea strikes you about how to solve your problem. Nature has given you an answer.

This scenario may not play out every time you get stuck at work. But I suspect it would happen more frequently than you might think if you would only give it the chance. Nature will speak to you of harmony, peace and stability. Nature is usually very predictable. It is in union with itself, and when you enter it consciously and deliberately, it welcomes you and enfolds you in its peace.

Managing Stress by Living Well

When you run smack into stress, you need some quick fixes. Fast. First, turn to calming down your body. Do some stretching exercises. Get a massage. Take a hot bath. Run, play tennis. Talk out your stress with a confidant.

Principle 13

Living a well and fit life is the best cure for stress.

Oftentimes, however, these quick efforts to overcome your stresses don't work too well. The reason is clear: If you are not in emotional, psychological and physical shape when stress throws its best punch, you will get knocked out. As I said near the beginning of this book, managing stress demands lifestyle changes. If you live your life fully and well, then when stress strikes you'll be ready for it. In fact, if you live fully, you will experience inner harmony and peace because you are living as your nature dictates. You will be totally fit. Or said another way: You will totally fit together.

Wellness is the antidote to stress. But wellness doesn't simply appear on the scene at the moment of stress and then leave, like Superman, until needed again. Wellness must be nurtured and given a full partnership in your life. It must go wherever you go – always.

Much of what I have addressed throughout this **Life Skills Series** touches important areas of wellness. But there are many other areas to consider. Although you and I cannot discuss all those areas in this book, I can, at least, give you a way of assessing your level of wellness and determining in which areas you need to work. By focusing on how *well* you are living, you will take your greatest strides toward reducing stress in your life. This is obviously a lifelong task. But it is one worth taking, because if you live well, you will fit together well. And you know, by now, that if you're *fit* you will live with little or no real stress.

"Wellness" has been a pop word in psychology for quite a few years. It's a fine word and has been useful. But in the context of this book and our understanding of stress in terms of things not *fitting*, I'd like to use the word *fit* instead of "well." So from now on we'll talk of "fitness."

Chapter Three

Assessing Your Fitness

By the simple act of reading this book and now taking the following self-assessment, you are already progressing on your way toward fitness. The most important element in your movement toward overall fitness is taking active charge of your own life. As you reach for a pencil to fill out this form, you are assuming responsibility for your own health.

Assessing fitness is one thing; establishing a clear and specific program of action is another; carrying out that program is the most demanding aspect of all. While your self-assessment will help you get a handle on your fitness project, in the final analysis you alone will make yourself fit. By doing so, you develop your most effective tool for reducing stress.

Notice that five major areas of fitness are identified:
1. Physical fitness.
2. Psychological fitness.
3. Social fitness.
4. Spiritual fitness.
5. Work-leisure fitness.

Each major area is described briefly, followed by a list of items in that category. After you look over each list, simply *underline* the items with which you are presently *dissatisfied.*

Once you have your list of "dissatisfied items," then number each item to rank it in the order that is most important for you to work on. Here is an example from the physical fitness portion of the assessment as filled out by one individual:

ITEMS

__ Smoking

1 Weight (too much, too little)

__ Energy (lack of, too much of)

3 Caffeine intake

__ Physical pain (chronic, intense)

2 Bodily tension (muscles, headaches, stomach problems)

DEFINE YOUR #1 PROBLEM

_____

_____

_____

_____

_____

_____

_____

_____

This person is most dissatisfied with "Weight" and so ranked it number one in importance. She ranked "Bodily tension" number two in importance to her and "Caffeine intake" third. Once she prioritized her list, she took her number one issue and defined it in the space provided. In this case, she wrote:

> *I continue to weigh more than I wish by about 15 pounds. I go on crash diets for a while and do well. Then I get discouraged because I don't see the weight dropping fast enough. I give up and begin eating more than I should. When I am overweight, my self-esteem falls badly. I get depressed and tend to eat even more. I want to stop this nasty cycle.*

Now you try it. In the pages that follow, first identify all the aspects of concern for you. Then rank them in terms of importance to you. Finally, take your highest-ranking item in that particular category and write out a description of the problem for you.

Physical Fitness

Physical fitness means feeling as healthy and vigorous and alive as possible. You need to know your personal and family history of illness and lifestyle. With that knowledge, you will be able to make good decisions about what health habits you need to work on. In addition, there are choices you can make that will carry you far beyond feeling "okay" to feeling great. You know yourself better than anyone else. You are the expert on you. Take a look now at these physical lifestyle patterns to evaluate your progress toward physical fitness.

DIRECTIONS:
1. Underline the items below with which you are not satisfied at the present time.
2. Then rank those underlined items according to the most important for you to work on.

ITEMS   **DEFINE YOUR #1 PROBLEM**

__ Smoking habits   _____

__ Present weight

__ Level of energy   _____

__ Caffeine intake

__ Level of physical pain   _____

__ Amount of bodily tension   _____

__ Sleeping patterns

__ Alcohol use   _____

__ Sexual desire & pleasure   _____

__ Body image

__ Eating & nutrition habits   _____

__ Use of medication

__ Frequency of exercise

__ Physical hygiene

Psychological Fitness

Psychological fitness begins with positive self-esteem. From that base you can develop thoughts that match reality and lead to constructive behaviors. Your healthy thoughts will also yield helpful emotions that bring security, contentment and joy. The task of psychological fitness is the integration of your thoughts, feelings and behaviors.

DIRECTIONS:

1. Underline the items below with which you are not satisfied at the present time.
2. Then rank those underlined items according to the most important for you to work on.

ITEMS	DEFINE YOUR #1 PROBLEM
__ Lack of creativity	
__ Lack of logical thinking	_____
__ Angry feelings	
__ Depressed feelings	_____
__ Over-sensitivity to others	_____
__ Hurt feelings	
__ Extended grief	_____
__ Unfree feelings	
__ Discontented feelings	_____
__ Mood swings	_____
__ Limited intuition	
__ Closed-mindedness	_____
__ Anxious feelings	
__ Fearful feelings	
__ Lack of self-confidence	
__ Lack of self-control	

(continued on next page)

__ Loss of memory
__ Lack of self-esteem
__ Low awareness of feelings
__ Inability to express feelings
__ Inability to meet my own needs
__ Feeling like a failure
__ Guilt feelings
__ Loneliness

_____

_____

Social Fitness

Focus here on your interpersonal relationships. "People contact" is to your psychological life what oxygen is to your physical life. Much joy and distress are caused by the ebb and flow of your interactions with people.

By looking at your most significant relationships, you can decide how to improve them. Developing goals in this area allows you to take greater control over your relational life. Relationships that work well always bring joy; those that don't work carry stress. Assess this area of your life by looking over the list of elements important to your relationships.

DIRECTIONS:

1. Underline the items below with which you are not satisfied at the present time.
2. Then rank those underlined items according to the most important for you to work on.

ITEMS   **DEFINE YOUR #1 PROBLEM**

__ Level of intimacy   _____

__ Reserved & shy feelings

__ Dishonesty   _____

__ Efforts to please others

__ Intolerance   _____

__ Self-revealing skills

__ Listening skills   _____

__ Inability to handle conflict

__ Lack of social graces   _____

__ Discomfort in conversation

__ Inability to say "no"   _____

(continued on next page)

__ Distrust of others
__ Unforgiving thoughts
__ Dependence on others
__ Excessive independence
__ Difficulty expressing needs
__ Disinterest in others
__ Difficulty expressing affection
__ Lack of sexual fulfillment
__ Relationship with
    __ Spouse
    __ Kids
    __ Parents
    __ In-laws
    __ Friends
    __ Men
    __ Women

_____

_____

Spiritual Fitness

Spiritual fitness involves the view you have of yourself as a member of this universe – and beyond. Your overall health is highly influenced by your beliefs regarding the meaning and purpose of life and death. Probably for you, as for the majority of people, these beliefs include the notion of a God or some transcendent power. Through these spiritual and, oftentimes, religious outlooks, you formulate your values and behaviors. Finally, your spiritual awareness serves as a cause of hope and yields a sense of direction in your life.

DIRECTIONS:
1. Underline the items below with which you are not satisfied at the present time.
2. Then rank those underlined items according to the most important for you to work on.

ITEMS   DEFINE YOUR #1 PROBLEM

__ Hopeless feelings

__ Lack of meaning & purpose   _____

__ Changing values

__ Lack of faith   _____

__ Doubts about spiritual things   _____

__ Inconsistency between reli-
    gious beliefs & daily life   _____

__ Attitude toward death   _____

__ Lack of prayer life

__ Doubts about afterlife   _____

__ Doubts about organized
    religion   _____

__ Lack of reflective time

_____

Work-Leisure Fitness

Fitness in this area means finding the proper balance of seriousness and playfulness. Most likely, work occupies a central place in your life and provides you with a sense of meaning and usefulness. It can be most fulfilling for you when it serves as a unique form of expressing your talents. It becomes a problem when it defines too completely who you are or regularly causes high levels of stress.

Your leisure activities can allow time for relaxation and play. They give you the freedom to "be" and not to "do." Leisure gives itself to you. It *fills* you up, whereas your work usually demands that you *give* to it. Striving to balance work and play contributes greatly to your overall fitness and health.

DIRECTIONS:

1. Underline the items below with which you are not satisfied at the present time.
2. Then rank those underlined items according to the most important for you to work on.

ITEMS   DEFINE YOUR #1 PROBLEM

__ Difficulty in setting priorities

__ Amount of work

__ Fear of taking risks

__ Lack of organization

__ Fast-paced lifestyle

__ Inability to relax

__ Inability to enjoy

__ Procrastination

__ Perfectionist ways

__ Adjusting to retirement

__ Problems managing money

__ Difficulty appreciating beauty
__ Job dissatisfaction
__ Inability to make decisions
__ Efforts at using my talents fully
__ Lack of meaning in work
__ Inability to play
__ Lack of goals in life

_____

_____

First Goals First

Now that you have identified elements of concern in the five major areas of fitness, choose the area that you believe you need to address first. All five are listed below. Please rank them – one through five – according to their importance to you. You will work first on the area that you rank number one; then you will work on the second ranked area and so on until you are functioning well in all five areas of your life.

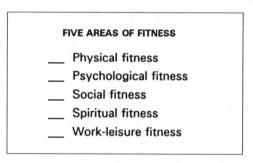

FIVE AREAS OF FITNESS

___ Physical fitness
___ Psychological fitness
___ Social fitness
___ Spiritual fitness
___ Work-leisure fitness

You've made your assessment and you've picked your first general area of concern. Now take the highest ranked specific issue and make a plan of action. Write out your plan. Make a chart if that helps. Talk to a friend, a confidant or a counselor to help you attack the problem area. Read, reflect and act according to your plan.

Getting fit will do more to reduce stress in your life than all the quick fixes you might hear about. If you are fit, you are in harmony with yourself. You will find inner peace because all the parts of you are balanced. I know it takes a lot of work and a good dose of perseverance to get fit. But being fit *is* the skill of managing your stress.

Chapter Four

Developing this Skill with Others

Becoming fit and managing stress demand considerable effort and staying power. You can get discouraged at times. You might not feel like remaining disciplined, or the temptations to seek immediate gratification might occasionally be too strong. It helps at times like these to have the support and encouragement of a friend or a group. Meeting regularly with another person or a group will definitely assist you in staying with your commitment to fitness.

Here are some steps you can take with another person or a group wishing to work on managing stress:

Step One

Begin by having everyone take the *assessment* presented in Chapter Three. Share the results within the group. Notice the similarities and the differences among the group members.

Step Two

Each of you can take your area of greatest concern and discuss the difficulty you are having with this aspect of your fitness.

Step Three

Talk about the *goals* each of you wants to achieve in your area of concern. Some of you may have the same goals, others not. For example, you might set a goal for yourself of doing the Relaxation Response once a day.

Step Four

Create an individual plan of action to reach your goal. Again, some of you may create similar plans, others may not. Everyone need not be working on the same issues. You want individuals in the group to take care of their *own* fitness project. By sharing goals and action plans, you can support one another.

Step Five

Go do it! Put your plan into action.

Step Six

Return to the group and report on your progress. Discuss pitfalls, rationalizations and failures as well as successes and achievements. Celebrate your *efforts*, not just the accomplishments. You can also discuss the insights you gained from readings you have done, conversations you've had with friends or a counselor on your subject, and so on.

Conclusion

This process can go on indefinitely. As you get a handle on your first area of concern, you can move on to your second area, and your third. Taking a specific area and working on it breaks down the overwhelming nature of fitness and gives you a way of grabbing onto the complex stresses that touch your life. Sharing these issues with others gives you the sense you are in this with other people who feel the same stresses as you do.

While the journey to a whole and fit life may sound difficult, it is filled with a physical and emotional charge that puts you on a higher plane of living. The rewards of becoming fit can only be known as you enter this life program. You will experience the sense of personal integrity, the feelings of accomplishment, and a vigor and dynamism that will make you say, "So, this is what life is all about!" You will know a deep inner harmony that comes from all parts fitting together.

Having developed the skill of managing stress, you will enjoy peace of mind and with it, I hope for you, a long, long life.

Appendix

Review of Principles for Managing Stress

1. Stress comes from three sources: personal, interpersonal and environmental.
2. Make a commitment to create harmony between your body and what you put into it.
3. Make a commitment to get physically active because your body needs it.
4. Practice relaxing your body regularly.
5. Develop a sense of confidence in your ability to cope with and reduce stress.
6. Realize that you cause your own stress by thinking suffering thoughts. To reduce stress, then, learn to think healing thoughts.
7. Learn when to say "no" and when to say "yes."
8. Reduce interpersonal stress by making your needs known.
9. Know when to resolve conflict and when to let it go.

10. To manage your time better, you need discipline.
11. Create a balanced lifestyle.
12. Respect and enjoy the earth and all that is in it.
13. Living a well and fit life is the best cure for stress.